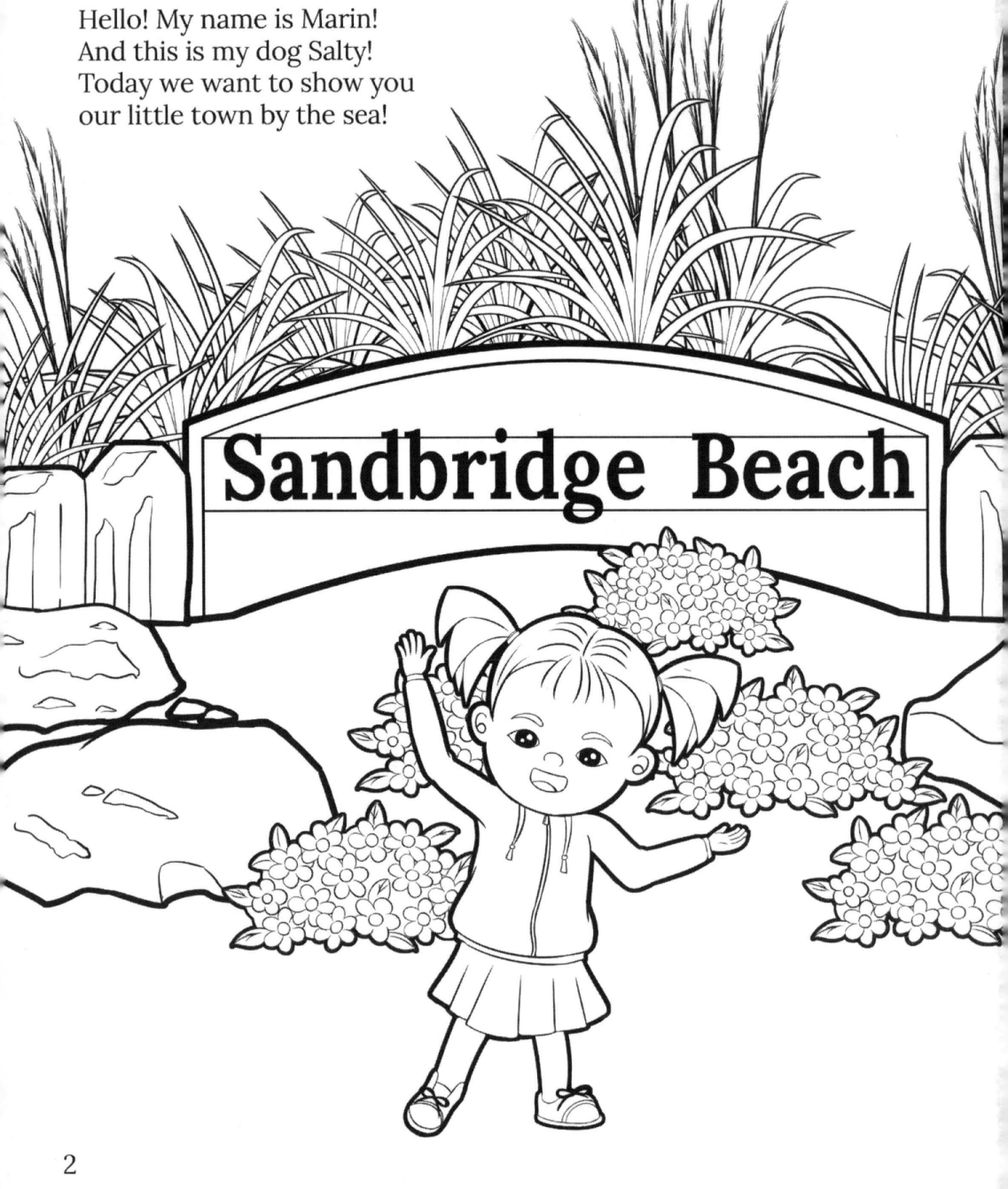

Sandbridge is a special place--
a place to love, live, and play--
a beautiful little town
between the ocean and the bay.

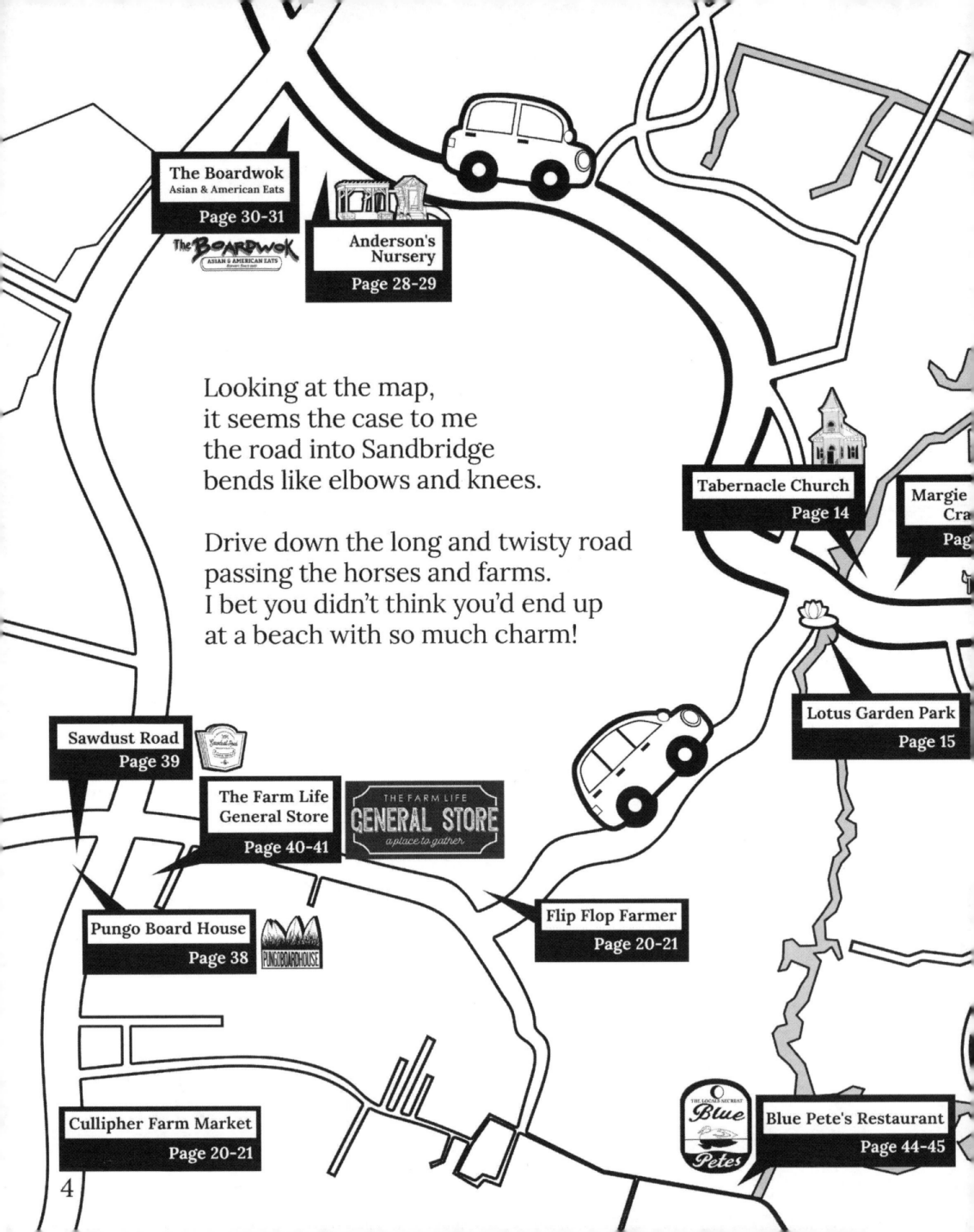

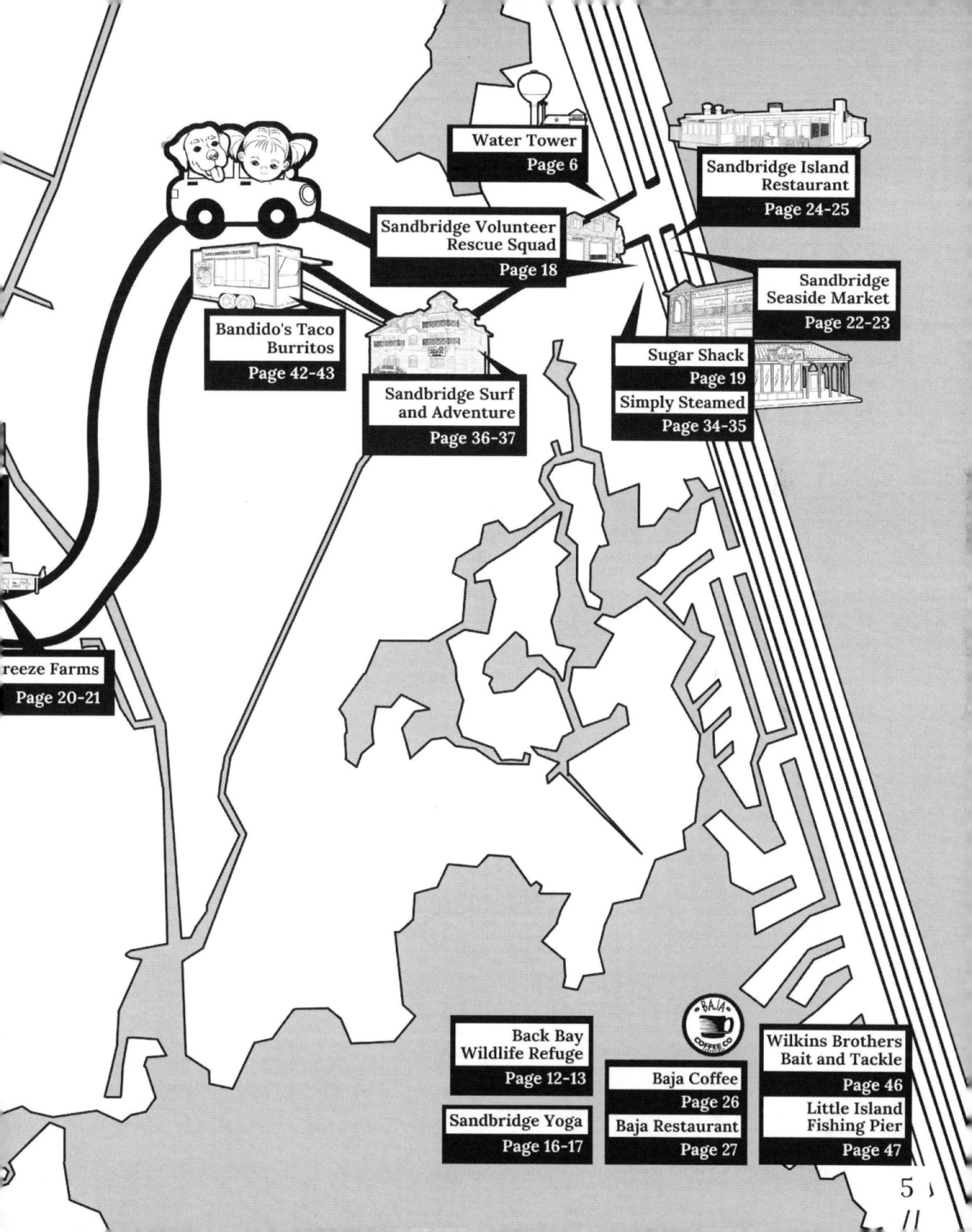

Welcome to Sandbridge!
Feel that sea breeze in your hair!
Take a look around Sandbridge Beach
and just smell that ocean air!

Let's make a plan
to maximize your fun
and hit all the best places in Sandbridge
before your trip is all done!

It's time to hit the beach!
Grab your towel, umbrella, and chair.
Are you ready for a day of fun
and playing without a care?!

Make sure to wear your hat
and put on the SPF.
When it comes to sun protection,
you really can't have enough!

If you go all the way down south,
go on a Back Bay hike.
You can park at the ranger office
or get there by riding bikes.

This is a wildlife refuge
meaning this place is protected.
Respect for the plants and animals
is what is expected.

Visit the Tabernacle Church, a true piece of history. The original structure was built way back in 1830.

If you'd like to stop in, it's a great opportunity for faith, fun, and fellowship in our community.

Start your day off with yoga.
Start it with a dose of zen.
Sandbridge Yoga offers classes with a view
to teens, women, and men!

Flow like the sea,
move like the bay.
Join us to find joy
and peace during your stay.

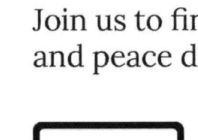

If your family is looking for some fun
at the end of the day's light,
head to the Firehouse's
now famous Bingo Night!

The money you spend
all goes to a great cause, you see.
It goes towards the Volunteer Rescue Squad--
keeping safe the Sandbridge community!

Sandbridge is most definitely a beach town but there are also lots of farms and market stands offering fresh produce, seafood, and treats from all across the surrounding lands.

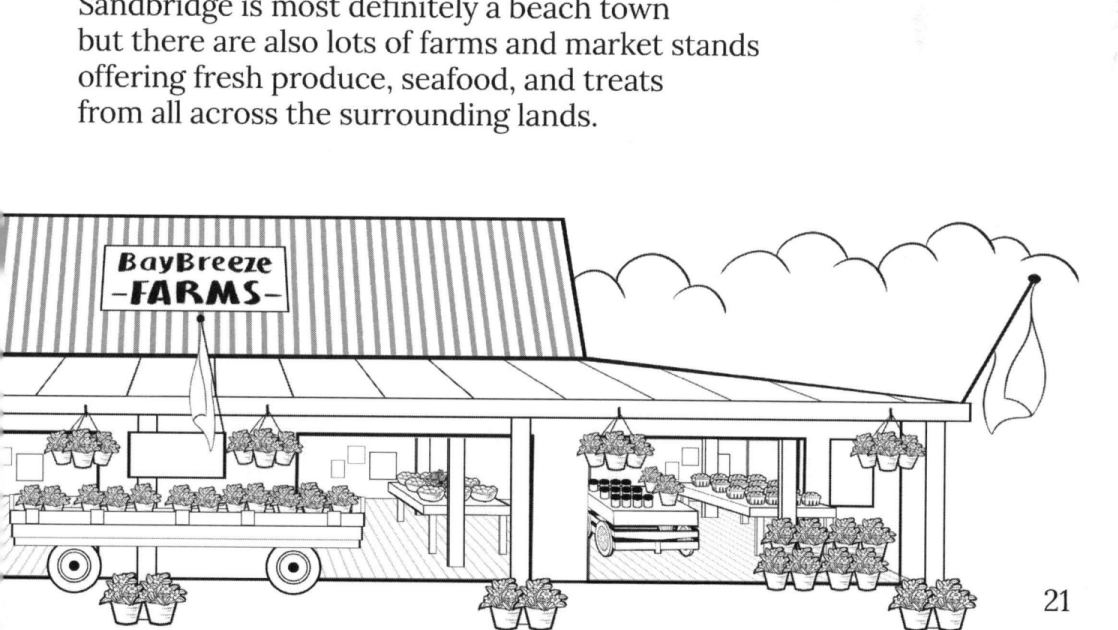

They bake them fresh daily
and there are lots to choose from.
My favorite has rainbow sprinkles...
would you like to try some?

Back behind the Market
is Sandbridge Island Restaurant
serving up fresh local foods
and all the pizza you want!

Order your food
and sit across from the dunes.
Relax with live music
and enjoy your food with some tunes!

We like to head down south
all the way to the end.
There, you will find Baja Coffee.
Poki will greet you as a friend.

Order a yummy breakfast
to fuel you up for your day.
Sip your coffee and eat your treat
with a beautiful view of the bay.

As the sun moves west
and the day turns to night,
head back out to the same spot.
Baja Restaurant is out of sight!

Kids line up to play dodgeball
or run around on the grassy lawn.
Everyone comes for the view and live music fun
and to watch the sun til it's gone.

There's a restaurant called Sage Kitchen
behind the greenhouse and store,
serving locally sourced and seasonal foods,
their menu offers yumminess galore!

You can play a round of mini golf
or on the playground all day.
At night, come for the fun live music
to complete your family's perfect stay!

Visit family-owned Boardwok .
They offer terrific Asian fare.
Everything's so good, you'll want to have it all.
Order lots of dishes and then share!

If you are lucky enough to visit
during the Chinese New Year,
check out their authentic performance.
You can only see it here!

Next door is Saw Dust Rd–
much more than just a coffee bar.
You will find an amazing breakfast,
coffee, art, and, often, a pop-up bazaar!

It's all handcrafted,
the coffee small batch.
From the food to the artwork,
it's all made from scratch!

Take a short trip across the street to visit The Farm Life General Store. Here, find local beef, produce, eggs, kombucha, and so much more!

If you are feeling like a good taco
then, mi amigo, you are in luck!
Bandidos has the absolute best
in Sandbridge's only food truck!

The tacos are so delicious!
The staff is friendly too!
Tell them we say hello
and that Marin and Salty sent you!

Some get here by boat
and some by the country roadsides.
Either way, Blue Pete's is known
for the food and fun it provides.

They provide an experience,
a true eating destination
for people who live here
and those on vacation.

Be sure to recycle; throw out your trash.
Take in all toys, chairs, and tents.
And as the saying goes:
"Leave only footprints."

But when it's time to pack up
with the slowly rising moon,
we hope you enjoyed your stay
and hope you come back soon!

Acknowledgements:

To my family. Thank you for being patient while Mommy writes her books. I love you so much Nick, Nicholas, Adria, Marin, and Salty.

To Salty, you are our family's hero. You are the best dock jumper, newspaper retriever, entire cod filet/Easter Ham/dark chocolate bar/sausage round stealer and eater. You have been demoted 3 times, grown old, and slowed down. But you are always up for an adventure, always want to be included, and just want to be with your pack. You are loyal, forgiving, and sweet, and the most patient creature on earth. Salty, you are the best!

To the Sandbridge residents, "it takes a village." Thank you for being our village.

Copyright © 2019 by Kimberly Naylor
Illustrated by Lei Yang

All rights reserved.

Travel Bug Press 2019
ISBN: 978-0-9979493-3-9